The Maverick Room

The Maverick Room

Poems

Thomas Sayers Ellis

Graywolf Press

Publication of this volume is made possible in part by a grant provided by the Minnesota State Arts Board, through an appropriation by the Minnesota State Legislature; a grant from the Wells Fargo Foundation Minnesota; and a grant from the National Endowment for the Arts, which believes that a great nation deserves great art. Significant support has also been provided by the Bush Foundation; Target and Mervyn's with support from the Target Foundation; the McKnight Foundation; and other generous contributions from foundations, corporations, and individuals. To these organizations and individuals we offer our heartfelt thanks.

Special funding for this title has been provided by the Jerome Foundation.

Published by Graywolf Press
250 Third Avenue North, Suite 600
Minneapolis, Minnesota 55401
All rights reserved.

www.graywolfpress.org

Published in the United States of America

ISBN 978-1-55597-414-5

4 6 8 9 7 5

Library of Congress Control Number: 2004109265

Cover design: Julie Metz

Cover photograph: *View of Slum Area with Capitol Building,* 1940
© Bettmann / Corbis
Interior photograph: Rare Essence Poster © Thomas Sayers Ellis

Monuments

My gratitude to the editors and readers of the following journals, anthologies, and newspapers in which these poems first appeared:

Agni, The American Poetry Review, Boston Book Review, Boston Review, Callaloo, Circular, Combo, Graham House Review, Grand Street, Hambone, Kenyon Review, Longshot, Ploughshares, The Southern Review, Tight, Tin House, WaxPoetics, American Poetry: The Next Generation, An Anthology of New (American) Poets, bum rush the page: a def poetry jam, Furious Flower: African American Poetry from the Black Arts Movement to the Present, Giant Steps: The New Generation of African American Writers, In The Tradition: An Anthology of Young Black Writers, Isn't It Romantic: 100 Love Poems by Younger American Poets, Legitimate Dangers: American Poets of The New Century, Making Callaloo: 25 Years of Black Literature, Poems, Poets, Poetry (Second Edition), Poet's Choice, Role Call: A Generational Anthology of Social and Political Black Literature and Art, The Discovery of Poetry, The Garden Thrives: Twentieth-Century African American Poetry, The New Young American Poets, The New American Poets: A Bread Loaf Anthology, 360: A Revolution of Black Poets, The Cleveland Free Times, Northern Ohio Live, The Philadelphia Inquirer, The Washington Post.

"A Baptist Beat" was reprinted in *Between God and Gangsta Rap* (Michael Eric Dyson, Oxford, 1996) and performed in *The Pocket* (dir. Nicholas Shumaker, Rolling Shin, 2002). "A View of the Library of Congress from Paul Laurence Dunbar High School" appeared in *The Washington Post* (*Book World,* May 6, 1996). "Atomic Bride" also appeared in *The Pushcart Prize XXII* (Pushcart, 1998) and *The Best American Poetry 1997* (Scribner, 1997). "Sir Nose D'VoidofFunk" was reprinted in the *Agni Document Series* #3 and in its limited edition pamphlet series. "Sticks" was performed in Furious Flower—Vol. IV: Initiates (California Newsreel, 1998). "T.A.P.O.A.F.O.M." appeared in *The Best American Poetry 2001* (Scribner, 2001).

"My Own—Stones" was written in response to *Bruce Nauman: 1985–1996, Drawings, Prints and Related Works* for the Cleveland Center for Contemporary Arts.

Some of these poems originally appeared in *The Good Junk* (*Take Three #1,* Graywolf Press, 1996) and *The Genuine Negro Hero* (Kent State University Press, 2001).

Special thanks to The Dark Room Collective. To Agnes Lee Hairston. To Charles H. Rowell and Askold Melnyczuk. To Amiri Baraka for inviting us to James Baldwin's funeral. To George Clinton and the P-Funk All Stars aka Parliament Funkadelic aka The U.S. Funk Mob for letting me ride. To my teachers S.H., D.W., and M.S.H. to whom I am eternally grateful. To the Ohio Arts Council, the MacDowell Colony, Yaddo, the Center for Book Arts (NYC), the Institute of Contemporary Art (Boston). The Boston Playwright's Theatre, Writers & Their Friends (Poets' League of Greater Cleveland). The Harvard Film Archive. The Fine Arts Work Center (Provincetown). To Jia, Joi, James and Fatima Cunningham, new kin. To my father, Sonny Boy, for making barbershops, record stores, and movie theaters all matter mo better than religion. To my contemporaries. To Tradition. To Seventh Street, you set me flowing. And to the ancestors, real and imagined, especially High John de Conquer, the original genuine negro hero.

for My Parents

NW

Starchild

for Garry Shider

Newborn, diaper-clad, same as a child,
That's how you'll leave this world.
No you won't die, just blast off.

Legs for rockets, bones separating like boosters.
Guitar: a lover, slanted in a hug, plucked,
Scratched, strummed. You will raise

One finger, on the one, for the one,
Then lift like a chorus of neck veins,
All six strings offering redemption.

The black hole at the center
Of the naked universe will respond
With a flash of light: comets, whistles,

Glowing noisemakers, bang, bang.
Roofs everywhere cracking, tearing,
Breaking like water.

Marcus Garvey Vitamins

a

All us we *folk*

person community first.

Invent truth,

b

no he didn't,

yes he *did*. Ain't English.

You *lyin'* to me.

c

Africa dis*agrees*

with subject-verb agreement.

Aspect ratio,

d

widescreen whiteache.

Don't like it, *don't* Pulitzer me.

I stress less than land*less*ness.

e

I break beat, I rhetorical strategy,

I escape route.

I, I, I, *psych.*

A Baptist Beat

A mixed congregation: sinners, worshippers,
Hustlers, survivors. All that terrible energy,
Locked in, trying to blend. Such a gathering
Of tribes has little, if any, use for a silk-robed choir.
Members bring their own noise, own souls.
Any Avenue Crew will tell you: nothing comes closer
To salvation than this. Here, there is no talk of judgment,
No fear. Every now & then, an uninformed god
Will walk in, bear witness, and mistake Kangol
For halo, and all those names for unwanted bodies
Being called home, arms raised to testify, waving
From side to side, fists flying like bullets, bullets
Like fists. Above the snare: two sticks make the sign
Of the cross then break—a divorced crucifix.
The tambourine shakes like a collection plate.
This pastor wants to know who's in the house,
Where we're from, are we tired yet, ready to quit?
We run down front, scream & shout, "Hell no,
We ain't ready to go!" The organ hesitates,
Fills the house with grace, good news, resurrection
& parole, a gospel of chords rising like souls.
Up, up, up up, down down. Up, up, up up,
Down. Up, up, up up, down down.
Up, up, up up, down. The cowbell's religious beat,
A prayer angel-ushered through dangerous air.

The Roll Call

Any half-decent rapper
Can conjure the dead,

Can reach into graves
And accuse God

Of Indian-giving.
The trick is ancestral,

No more magic than memory's
Hidden strings & chains.

Trust me,
We haven't forgotten a name.

Say them. Raise your hands.
Holler at me!

A Pack of Cigarettes

Being in a group
—a good one—could
make you
so cool you smoked.

Wilson Pickett

I started cooking
on the road
because of segregation.

Smokey Robinson

I

So what
if they were
hoodlums,
George Clinton's gang: The Outlaws
never stole

nor seriously
hurt anyone.
All they did was croon
on corners
and break curfew

—press police
records, one breathtaking
release after another.
No violence
until nicotine hit

with the same
discriminating coffin nails
as segregation.
Airplay limited
to the whole notes

of smoke
Parliaments made before rumbles,
Jim-Crow*ded*.
All three lungs negro
as vinyl. Low

      tar and pompadours,
third-degree burns.
Car groups versus bird groups.
Doo conks wop.
Fire Department right next door

      and barbershop CLOSED.
No wonder The Outlaws
had nowhere to run,
after graduation,
except

      the needle-patrolled,
bald highways
between
pretty silky black
songs.

    2

      A band backing singers
backed by singers
backing a band.
Show each other up.
Who smoke

who don't
never inhale, squares.
Habits common as demos.
As shotguns.
As coughs.

      Scratched instrumental side
of 45 way more live
than vocal. Arrangement:
help each other out.
To prevent cancer

    learn rhythm before lead.
Shoot up, relax, nod and nap.
Inject Marshall amps.
Also, blow enough score
acid enough

      to speed smack down,
just don't forget
to give the funky
triflin' junky drummer
some

    of his own uncut skin to stick
then sight-fix Eddie and Tawl
a whole 'nother yard of tongue
more souled out
than auditioning

        black butts bent
standing straight up.
Nice suits now nigger, niggerer, niggerish
as the psychedelic,
ghetto-metal,

    gypsy-baptist,
sky-church Motown wasn't.
A tobacco-enema for young America.
Breath tampons
last longer.

Sticks

My father was an enormous man
Who believed kindness and lack of size
Were nothing more than sissified
Signs of weakness. Narrow-minded,

His eyes were the worst kind
Of jury—deliberate, distant, hard.
No one could outshout him
Or make bigger fists. The few

Who tried got taken for bad,
Beat down, their bodies slammed.
I wanted to be just like him:
Big man, man of the house, king.

A plagiarist, hitting the things he hit,
I learned to use my hands watching him
Use his, pretending to slap mother
When he slapped mother.

He was sick. A diabetic slept
Like a silent vowel inside his well-built,
Muscular, dark body. Hard as all that
With similar weaknesses

—I discovered writing,
How words are parts of speech
With beats and breaths of their own.
Interjections like flams. Wham! Bam!

An heir to the rhythm
And tension beneath the beatings,
My first attempts were filled with noise,
Wild solos, violent uncontrollable blows.

The page tightened like a drum
Resisting the clockwise twisting
Of a handheld chrome key,
The noisy banging and tuning of growth.

Nicknames

for Darrell Haley

> We must learn to wear our names
> within all the noise and confusion
> of the environment in which we find ourselves;
> make them the center of all our associations
> with the world, with man and with nature.
> We must charge them with all our emotions,
> our hopes, hates, loves, aspirations.
> They must become our masks and our shields
> and the containers of all those values
> and traditions which we learn and/or imagine
> as being the meaning of our familial past.
>
> *Ralph Ellison*

We could signify.
Any twin was Twin.
The shape of Moe's head
made him Dick,
slang for the male organ.
Darryl was Tee Tee,
the asthmatic noise
he made whenever
he ran. Anybody
with a limp, Crip.

Girls had it worse.
Feel sorry for Tawana,
so short so brown
she was called Roach.
Also Ernestine, better known
as Teeny Weeny
because she was
flat-chested and had
a small behind
like a boy's.

My man Meat
wanted to box. Boo, coach.
Poobie, design clothes.
What stopped them?
Whatever.
Andre's dark side,
Drako, got him locked up.
Black Eddie was shot
in the back by a cop
during a holdup.

Go Ju *go* Ju *go*.
Lightskinned Rainbow
eclipsed Tick Tock,
his chocolate walk-partner.
Incestuous Pinkie and Tan.
Both Frogs. Squirrel. Crazy ass Sponge.
Bama Duke's lopsided,
sticky daughter, Peaches.
Our b-shaped barber,
Blinky. We miss you,

Missy, rest in peace.
John Rocks-on-Rocks.
The Young Dillingers.
Freckles versus Baby Tim.
Cabalou stuttering,
i-m-m-mi-t-ta-ting Johnny Lips.
Hillbilly, Lefty, Itchy and Skip.
Dootie Bug's first
baby's mama, leaving.
Tootie had Fin.

Lucky lucky me: Sayers
because I was fast
and Sticks because I was skinny.
Spanish Doug. Erno. Shoe and Ding.
The Immaculate Conception
and Gibson Plaza Apartments
double-baptizing poverty.
Oldhead Jimbo spoiling
healthy baby girls
Stuff or Boo.

Born busy and still busy,
our restless senses typecast
Jerry Green as Dirty Jerry,
Fat Dave as himself
and all four Lightfoots as Light.
Alcohol took Redbone
from Redds & The Boys.
Reader, you figure
Kerry's mama's
dozen for Mess.

Imagine, then, the scars
spared flawed iris Dot-Eye
and Heavy-One's inability to dodge
the percussive dice roll
of random gunfire.
Cherry trees that blossom,
blister and bleed.
God's called upon
home-ruled hands,
pocketing Footz.

That Fuss Was Us

Notice! Stop! Help Save the Youth of America!
Don't Buy NEGRO RECORDS. The screaming,
idiotic words, and savage music of these records
are undermining the morals of our white youth
in America. Call the advertisers of the radio stations
that play this type of music and complain to them!
Don't let your children buy, or listen to these
Negro records.

from a poster reproduced
in front of the Parliament Tour book

The Chocolate Jam,
R.F.K. Memorial Stadium,
Washington, D.C. (1977)

The eye
atop the
pyramid

means

peek-
a-boo,

means

we've been
watching
you,

guard up,

defend
yourself,

means

we shall
overcome,

means

you go
tell it,

we've
already
been to
the mountain
top,

no need
to reinvent
humps,

means

we paid
for the flying saucers,
extraterrestrials
and maggots

our damn
god selves,

not an
album cover penny
from
Casablanca,

17

not a
folded dollar bill
from
Westbound,

means

pay attention,

means

IN FUNK
WE TRUST
NO ONE

except

THE ONE.

Stretchin' Out

for William "Bootsy" Collins

The whole
        hard thumb
followed
    by the weight
        of the hand
        (all nineteen
bones and
        then some),

thrusting
   and slapping—
      a snake charmer
   taming a snake.
This is the
way he funks
   with you,
blow by blow
   backwards—part
      under a sheet,
   part out in
     the open,
   so you can't
see what he's
doing. Not just
   another funky
bass, not just
   another friendly
     phone fanatic,
   but Bootzilla—
the world's
only
   Rhinestone
Rockstar
  Monster
    of a doll
  baby. A
chocolate star,
   he just wants
to satisfy,
to put your booty
  to duty,
  to make the whole
joint stand,
   to stretch *it*
way out

like
  a
rubber
  band.

Fuzzy Finds a Bible

for Clarence Haskins

For years they
monitored the hairs
on his funk
—the move from
Potter's Crossing
to living with cousins
in Plainfield, getting
his hair processed,
doowopping with George,
Calvin, Grady & Ray.

It didn't surprise them
when he broke his neck,
straddling and gyrating
with the microphone,
People, what you doing?

Somehow they knew
he'd be the first one
on the P-Funk Earth Tour bus,
down from the high of rehearsal,
exhausted and delirious,
a bearded buccaneer,

knew body memory
would send him to the back,
top left bunk, where it lay,
leather-bound, radioactive,
a hit single, red hot, your momma,
knew he'd climb in bed
with it, enter holiness
—that he'd confuse,
not only his role onstage
with his role on earth,
but its words with his own.

It became a part
of his nappy,
like permanence, like stash,
Chocolate City-to-city,
dressing room-to-dressing
room, stage.

            They even knew
he'd quit the Funk Mob
on a June night
in the City of Angels
far from his mother's call,
far from home.

The extraterrestrial brothers
who put it there,
put it there for a reason.
The fear of God,
like Funk,
rewards its own.

Big Foot Music

for Glenn Goins (1954–1978)

Nobody
vomits church
basement
like Glenn, his
    last supper
was Sunday,
    leftover
            hamhocks &
cornflakes.

What's so nasty
    about funky food,
ashy kneecaps & rusty ankles?

His last bowel
movement was lumpy
    gravy,
toilet paper
    on a stiff
    middle finger.

Testifying is contagious,
upsets the stomach,

    constipates hate. *You*

            see Jesus
    is his
airplane. *You see*

Jesus
is hot grits on
Al Green

and Richard Pryor on fire.

You see Nobody hears as many
Amen
as Glenn.

Even here,
in the studio,
the right arm rises
to shield his eyes

as if
he sees something
or someone other Funks don't.

Please help him
get rid of some of this.

I know what you
can do.
Lord,

make
him a plate. He
looks queasy,
about to faint.

If James Brown
could just see
            him now,
giving up food for
   funk, way down, P
      below D,

doing life to death,

   body

        trembling like a witness,
religious as motion,
            them hips.

NE

Zapruder

Day off in dark suit and hat,
looking through the viewfinder
of a new eight millimeter Bell & Howell camera,
paying no mind the open windows, the seizure.
Just how more than half the targets on the grassy knoll
are potential customers, models, women,
how accident and aim could fit them all,
including the car, into frame. It was the sixties,
so before the volume of the motorcade
turned north up Houston then down on Elm,
they passed the camera between them like a joint,
a silent investment. His secretary stood next to him,
confident that their film would change lives,
that what the women wore to greet the president
would influence their sewing machines and needles.
Clicking the power on added something
above and below human to autumn. Now comes history,
that moment when everything begins to wave:
arms, flags, lens, minutes, seconds, silence,
dressmaker, souvenir, evidence.

Barracuda

for Anthony Jordan,
former member
of the Paul Laurence Dunbar High School
Barracudas Swim Team

Your memory of water
is clouded by a crimson tide,
sad bulging eyes,
a dive—headfirst
into pages of chlorine.
The past evaporates
into a silence that floats,
corpselike, on its side.
At Dunbar, we did time
on our backs and the water,
though friendlier,
was less penetrable
—like the sky, a master
of reflected disguises.
There must be a word
for what you're doing.
Are you crying?
Damp days.
Solitudes crowded with loneliness.
Years swim before you.
Memory moves like sewage
through the brain's plumbing.
With a cadaver of guilt
on your back,
you've done so many push-ups
the stripes on your chest
are stronger than bars.
You're inside yourself,
examining bubbles for answers.

28

Your body's a cell,
the cell's a tank.
Yet nothing, save time,
passes through you.

Slow Fade to Black

for Thomas Cripps

and in memory of The Lincoln, The Republic
& The Booker T. Theaters,
formerly of U Street, N. W.

Like a clothesline of whites
Colored hands couldn't reach,
a thousand souls crossed
promised air and the screen glowed
like something we were supposed
to respect & fear. Daylight
& Sunday were outside,
waiting to segregate darkness
with prejudices of their own.
A silhouette behind a flashlight
led us down an aisle
into The Shadow World,
rows & rows of runaways
awaiting emancipation.
Theater, belly, cave,
ate what got in.
We half dreamt weightlessness,
salvation, freedom, escape.
A resurrection of arms,
we wished were wings,
reached in & out of greasy buckets
picking something the precise
color & weight of cotton.
Just above heads,
Pam Grier & Richard Roundtree
dodged bullets
and survived falls from as high
as heaven—miracles

not worth building
dreams on. And like an ampersand
between eyes & ears,
the soundtrack strung
together images
the way popcorn butter & soda syrup
held us to earth.

Sir Nose D'VoidofFunk

[1]

That name: D'VoidofFunk.
An expressionistic thing

With do-loops
And threes in it,

Preceded by
A silly-serious

Attempt by
Old Smell-O-Vision

To cop
Some nobility.

[2]

The whole bumpnoxious,
Dark thang stanks
Of jivation

And Electric Spank.
Glory, glory, glory-
hallastoopid.

Then there's his funny
Accent—pitch
Change and delay

Looped through
Feedback, pre-spankic
Self-satisfunktion.

Nose gets harder
As his voice
Gets higher.

Nose won't take
His shoes off,
Dance, swim or sweat.

Nose snores,
A deep snooze,
Snoozation.

[3]

Syndrome tweedle dee dum. Despite
The finger-pointing profile,
False peace signs
And allergic reaction

To light, we brothers
Wanna be down
With Nose. All that!
The girls, the clothes.

Now you know Nose
Knows when to fake it
And when to fake
Faking it.

      Waves
Don't mean he's gone
Or that there's going
To be a cover-up,
Very Nixonian.

You can't impeach Nose.
Where's your courtroom,
your wig and robe?
You ain't Nose judge.

Somebody scream just to see
The look on our party's
Tromboneless face,
That burial ground

Of samples and clones
Jes grew. A nose
Is a nose is a nose
Is a nose,

                    so
Wherever the elephants
In his family
Tree untrunk
Is home.

    [4]

And that's about the only tail
Mugs can push or pin
On him.

Spellbound

for Tracy K. Smith

The balcony is filled
with couples wondering,
If and how long the hypnosis
will last? Psychotherapy & light
versus darkness, an underground railroad
of hope. Escape,

is that what we're here for?
Eyes glued to the screen have no
better sense of which star to follow
than the blind heart. Peck & Bergman kiss,
and doors open that we are not
allowed to see close. Emptying,

an orgy of voyeurs strains
itself through a glass of milk,
a third & thicker lens. Interpretation
of what? The screen goes white,
a cow's stomach turned inside out.
I'd hate to think of slaughter,

lovers at the mercy
of an omniscient somnambulist,
that the brain is a Hollywood filmmaker
crazy with cameras. Odd isn't it,
how if we wore eyes & ears on our chests
we'd have more respect for the heart.

Glory

                                    At Old Sturbridge,
a rooster's bark helped lift darkness
back up, beyond angels & smoke, to where
all things, regardless of size & color,
weigh the same. A slipcover of dew
camouflaged blades no longer green enough
to hurt, and three hundred uniformed extras

played possum, fallen blue & grey stars
against a sky of grass, war's constellation
of bodies & limbs. The director yelled
"Quiet!" & "Action!" And the black men
we'd cast as gravediggers walked toward us.
No more than actors told what to do,
a dark cloud unable to ignore God.

It didn't take much to make Boston's South End
look like Beacon Hill—top hats, overcoats,
dewinged confetti, American flags draped
like smiles over the frowns of brownstones.
The regiment marched through, principals standing in.
My friend Noland was next to Morgan Freeman,
but the cinematographer knew how to frame a shot,

how to exclude a man with a camera.
Francine Jamison-Tanchuck was there,
stitching cloth to celluloid. A natural-born seer,
her hands hid matrimony & promise in hoop dresses
      & bonnets
so that each soldier witnessed a flash of cross
& ring, a small church, heaven on earth,
things thought worth fighting for.

Undressing Mr. Wiggles

for Overton Loyd

A semibionic
irreducible commodity,
both hit and splash
and metafoolish
as red panties and fins
on letterforms—all drawn
under the influence
of seaweed, reason
for the tank harmonics,
bubbly vocalizations
and liquid licks.
All graffilthy.

      Your funkentelechy
      gave birth to the nation.

Overseer of wiggling blackness,
first line dance and final splank.
Antitour all antiwar.
Off the hook, hooked and a hook.
Not hung or hung up
on earholes, clothes, clones,
or his own bones
like some kissed egos
we know. Pure woo.
Throbassonic wetness and perfection.
Life force and downstroke.
Deep togetherness.

      The potential existence
      of a nation is to rise.

All-night crazoid craving for liquid sunshine.
Finger-in-their-hole
and non-profish from day one.
Boptist and blowpole.
Only yo-yo and wheels
not in fatigues and sync.
Go wiggle or go skate.
Only bait no feet to fail him.
Just the skin and swim he's in
and the swim and skin
skins hit him in.
A Vaseline victory.

    A man with no imagination
    has no wet dream.

Black Freekdom: Suzie Thundertussy, Octavepussy
and the Motor-Booty Girls,
Giggles and Squirm.
Something stank and the yellow bird
above concert ate some.
Ring-around-the-record companies.
Small musty halls
instead of large, sold-out ones.
Butt-to-butt resuscitation.
The magic rhythm
by which all defunkatized juices
become revitalized.
Butterflyworms.

    Album cover your ears
    and come in and throw down.

My Autopsy

The Man in the Dark Room

for Ellen Gallagher

My eyes are women surrounded by lesbian graves.

My eyes come together and kiss like knees.

My eyes twist and cross like some strange head.

My eyes dance the fandango like fish feet
In kitty litter.

My eyes sleep in two dark rooms under a shaved
And uncombed universe. My eyes are sisters.

I sent my eyes to space and they came back
Explored to tears, rejected by rent-controlled
Black holes.

Next, I'm sending them to sea.

A Shaved and Uncombed Universe

My hair grows an inch—I too am a world.
Theodore Roethke

The ink is still on yesterday's pancakes,
A bag of vitamins under my eyes.

The October moon is a deformed egg
With a premature sun inside.

39

My eyes are jealous because I shaved my head
To make room for more ears.

On the milky expressway to lunch,
I passed the earth still standing in line for breakfast.

I am the center of the universe.
All other planets pretend and renege.

There isn't a civilized tooth in my mouth.
They have all been buried inside my head too long.

The earth is a poorly tossed stone
That keeps coming in third.

When I shake the sky,
Hot dandruff falls.

All the secrets of the universe, mine first,
Dismantled and realized as reservoirs of ink
For all to drink from.

Stars on my shoulders
Like atomic breath.

Hush Yo Mouf

for Bob Kaufman

I

Pretty soon, the Age of the Talk Show
Will slip on a peel left in the avant-gutter.

2

I refuse to write for more people
Than I can listen to.

3

I tripped over a tongue last night
And failed to wipe up the metaphors.

4

The world is held together by the word
Of one person who ignores everybody.

5

The Space Race is foolish;
NASA will never catch up with Sun Ra.

6

Since Virginia Beach, I've added Heckle and Jeckle
To my list of endangered mythical beasts.

7

My father and I have my mother in common.
She does all the talking.

8

A slap in the face is the most corrective form of punctuation,
Sentencing.

9

Bomb coffee houses, not abortion clinics.

10

The preachers of plasma say Give the gift of life,
Rhetoric.

11

Talk, talk, talk.
Lies, lies, lies.

12

A thousand pubic persons, all publicly pissant, politicians.

14

Talk, rumor, he say she say, word of mouth,
History.

15

Wanted Dead or Aloud
Someone to rinse the tongue stuff from my eyes

16 .

I, too, write writing

17

(We bony Vs
Trying to make a W)

18

And drink ink.

19

Child, *please*.

20

I came to this planet to escape walkie-talkies.
I failed.

The Maverick Room

for The Whole Damn Crew

go-go, (noun) 1. to go for it *[Fr. early Motown; poss. Yoruba "agogo"]*. 1. A vernacular dance music unique to Washington, D.C.; a non-stop, live party music in which a pulsing bass drum beat blends with African rhythms and the sounds of timbales, cowbells, and conga drums as trumpets, trombones, saxophones and synthesizers belt out licks from Jazz, Funk and Soul, punctuated by rapped greetings to the local crews and ongoing dialogue between the dance floor and the band;

2. a music/dance event featuring Go-Go bands, generally at a community center, skating rink or dance hall, frequented by teens and young teens "hooked up" in the latest in casual wear; (verb, int.). 1. To go for it.

I *The Break of Dawn*

Explosive posters lit at night.
On every tree a cardboard saviour
Nailed to rooted echoes of wooden agony.

Sidewalks graffitied with chalk silhouettes,
Stank of murder, scabs of moonlight
Patch our wounded night.

Wrapped in bandaged blue, pale morning
Wakes the day. Mute doses
Of evaporating darkness on the breath of potholes.

II *Cowbell*

You're how we found The Maverick Room,
The Cave Yard, The Black Hole and block parties
In hard-to-find inner-city neighborhoods
With names like Congress Heights and Valley Green.

You're the Real McCoy,
What we used to teach timid beginners to hit back.
When the power went out you gathered kin,
A family discussion of percussion.

Tambourine, vibra-slap, ratchet.
We met reaching into the same pocket,
Agreed a crowded one is equivalent to sin.
Sticks can't harm the real you.

You're what gets heard,
A prayer above crowd noise and soul.
Down-to-earth, hardheaded, hollow, loud.
I know your weak spots. You know mine.

III *Giant Steps*

Sugar Bear is the Abominable Snowman of Go-Go,
Laying stone-cold sheets of bottom
Over forgotten junk farms and Indian deathbeds.

Years ago, a conspiracy to melt him
Was put to sleep by an unlimited freeze.

He bridged the gap between Southeast & Northwest,
Passing through Anacostia and Watergate,
Untouched, plucking veins & exposing hidden tapes.

Bear's melody is Big Foot music;
2 places at the same time.

On atomic nights
His footprints can be viewed from heaven,
Extinguishing mushrooms.

Bear let the first fox loose on the moon.
Hear his cry: *ooh la la la!*

IV *On Display*

A ghost with PCP eyes
Bops through my memory.

Her skirt rises as she
Spins through love boat,

Lagerfeld & hot breath. *Up*
Against the wall standing

Very tall, he's got the big
Spotlight and he's doing it all.

We playact black ants surround-
ing a crumb, then go at her

Like a broken drumroll bang-
ing silence. Six, seven,

Nine, straight through her.
Turn off the house lights y'all,

Says James Funk, *so we can put*
Everybody on display.

Aw turn off the house lights
Y'all, so we can get everybody

On display. Aw get it!

V *Take Me Out to the Go-Go*

Little Benny zips across stage
Trailed by a troop of white-gloved
One-wheelers: Killer Joes,
The 12 & Under Crew
In disguise.

A sixth sense guides him
Beyond darkness. An
Inner voice says when,
Don't stop, don't stop, don't stop,
I'll tell you when.

A constellation of funeral homes.
Jumpsuits. Red & white
Ribbons in the sky. The total
Groove, a carnival of roses
Circling the moon.

Mere call & response
Never knocked socks this way,
Lifting nicknames & dates
From the faces of tombstones
And mere call & response never will.

God climbs inside,
Asking for souls—
Something we weren't taught to share.

VI *The Moonlite Inn*

I

Our truck rolled out of an alley
In Petworth at 8—after dinner,
A bellyful of roadies & chrome.
Like a compass, a cracked cowbell sat
On the dashboard, its black mouth a contradiction,
One lip curled North, the other South
Like a griot's or seashell's. Young Boy
Doubled as driver & navigator—
A dirty windshield like a veil,
The only thing between him & myth.

2

Suburbia was mysterious,
Calmer, less poetic. The homes were armless,
Flat & wide, and unable to reach up
Or out like most prose. Stars hid
Like schools of truant fish,
The headlights in their moist skulls
Blinking off & on, distress signals,
Gossip from God. A cop's flashlight
Stood in for the moon,
A navel holding together heaven.

3

After we cranked
Ayre Rayde grooved and the ladies
We thought had come to see us
Drifted beyond our reach. That night
Names & numbers were exchanged,
Directions drawn on the blank maps
Of palms. Also, something as out
Of reach as dawn broke in us
And our shadows tried to climb sky
The wrong way down.

VII *Block Party*

A permit is obtained
In advance. Orange, fluorescent
Pylons are placed in the middle
Of the street at both ends
Of the block. No thru traffic,
Nowhere to park.

Weather allows
Word to spread like
A sexually transmitted disease.
Streetwise, one big
Virus, bacon grease,
The epicenter of an itch.

Expect groove, good junk,
Chitlin' buckets. The DJ is
Too old to be still
Living at home,
Every summer turning
His mama's front yard

Into a radio station.
A garden of plastic crates,
Wax irises, small reels
Of weeds, two turntables
And a microphone,
Headphones flipped forward

Like the face guard
On a football helmet.
Spin doctor, athlete, star.
Expect old folks, night
Owls perched on porches,
Peering out dark windows.

Expect youngins,
Ripping and running,
High on sugar, salt, sun.
Sodas, burgers, dogs. Bass booming,
Booming again, and backing
Away like thunder.

A synthesized bomb
Parts the crowd. Roadies
In flare-red jumpers
Work like hustlers,
Plugging things in
And taking things out.

A sea of us wave
And go *ho,* pumping
Our fists like fists.
The street stretches like skin,
Curbs distant as shores,
Rival congregations, storms.

VIII *Tapes*

for Nico Hobson

We got them the hard way,
Taking turns holding recorders
Blessed with the weight of D batteries

On our shoulders.
We pressed PLAY & RECORD,
Ready to release PAUSE

The moment the drummer
Flexed visible muscle
Or the synthesizer whined

Like a siren.
Weren't we lucky
A few clubs had balconies.

I remember the red lights,
How we looked up
When Robinson frisked us.

We made copies,
Refusing to trade the ones
With our names on them,

Came to blows
When one was lost, stolen.
"Make me a copy,"

Carmichael said
The day after his brother's murder.
A way of remembering,

Holding on.
Ranked next to gold chains
& school clothes,

Our love for them
Was southern—the older ones
Getting the most

Attention.
Care.
Respect.

IX *Shooting Back*

for Mr. G

You load, focus, aim.
The shutter falls like a tiny axe,
Reopens, a blinking eye washed in light.

An image enters the world
Premature, wet, lit like a miracle. The holier ones
Exploit darkness, develop like secrets.

Only the faithful possess
Nerve enough to stand this long, arms crossed,
Fearlessly posed, in the line of fire.

Every shot attempts to capture
The will-to-survive of its target:
High-top fades, hooded sweats, hard stares,

A Gucci background, a wicker chair.

X *Stalking Another Man's Hands*

for David Green

I trained mine
  To move like yours.
    I stood behind

A row of silver & black rototoms,
  Twisting and tuning
    And mimicking

Your body moves
  As if they were my own.
    My bad.

I wore fake gold,
  Dress shoes with shorts
    And shiny shirts

Wide open,
  Flipping & spinning my sticks
    Fast as propellers

So the tip the top,
  The top the tip would disappear.
    I took time out,

To do-the-do,
  To do-it-fluid,
    To do-it-on-down

And sho nuff sho nuff
  Freakbodies wanted me
    Right there in the socket,

So I taped my fingers
　　And rolled my sleeves
　　　　And pretended I was you.

Heap big,
　　Heap big,
　　　　Heap big fun

All up-inside Celebrity Hall
　　Where Lisa-of-the-World
　　　　Wrote my name next to hers

And the sweet Jesus
　　You gave your recent ex
　　　　Clung to my chest

(The same night Miss Mack
　　Suspended you)
　　　　Like a child nailed to a swing.

Uh-oh,
　　Uh oh-oh,
　　　　Uh-oh.

The bridge.
　　C-natural debris.
　　　　The pocket beneath the bridge.

Wop wop
　　Shoo be. Shoo be
　　　　Doo wop.

You're half responsible
    For my first abortion. You're half responsible
        For my first born.

No ins & outs.
    No recording devices.
        No refunds.

A bop,
    Be bop bop. A bop,
        Be bop bop.

SW

A Kiss in the Dark

In our community everything was kept quiet,
behind closed doors. When dogs got stuck
it was because one was hurt and the other
was a friend, helping it home—just like a friend.
Once Reverend Gibson ran from the church
with a bucket of hot water, and when it separated them,
they sang. That's why it was such an event,
a mistake equivalent to sin, when my parents
left their bedroom light on, door open.

Mistakes are what gave light to that tiny apartment
darkness tried to conquer. And imagination,
how there had to be more to it than
the quick & crude *He put it in and he took it out.*

A naked bulb on the dresser next to where
they made me made them celebrities, giants, myth.
I watched their black shadows on the wall,
half expecting fade-out and something romantic
as the final scene of *Love Crazy,* my father
a suave William Powell, my mother's slender body
a backwards C in the tight focus of his arms—
close shot, oneiric dissolve and jump cut to years
before their separation and the arrival of hot water.

Photograph of Dr. Funkenstein

after Christian Witkin

A crazy evil grin, eyelids flipped
Inside out, red hot and pink as pork.
The tongue slipping out the mouth
Suggests fellatio, and a pussy taunting dogs.

He is arrested, in custody,
MOST WANTED, an atomic shaman
With a scratch and sniff beard. I'll bet you
He was dreaming of Venus, about to say something nasty
When the photographer bopped him
With a nickel bag of light into a permanent
Type nod, sizzaleenmean, somewhere
Between a mugshot and maximumisness.

Judging from the shirt and tie,
He's well hung and may have been
About to make a house call (reach
Way up and give Sir Nose a splanking
Or photosynthesize, a dandy lion)
When the booty snatchers slapped him
With a warrant, shoving him, handcuffed,
Onto a death row of commodes,

A zone of zero funkativity,
Violating his right to hold
His own thang, his right to pee.

View-Master

for you, mother, thanks

I guess
I got it
from you,

this habit
of clenching
my face
into a fist,

this brutal
looking into,

your way
of seeing things,

squinting,

one eye
clearly unable
to reach
as far as
the other.

A childhood
plagued
by headaches

from straining
and watching
far too
much TV,

up close,

so nothing
would escape.

Then at ten
I got an
inexpensive gift,

one that held
images up

closer to
my face
like a kiss.

Imitating
the kids
who were
supposed to be
friends,

I blinked
and blinked,

testing
my sight with it
—perfect vision
in my right eye,

but the left one
was weaker.

It backed away,

watered
then blurred.

Farsighted!

your doctor
proclaimed,

adding windows

to our already
veiled corner
of the world.

We left linked,
two good eyes
between us,

joined by
our shared flaw.

You passing
your gift,

me making myth
with it.

Bright Moments

for Globe Poster Printing Corporation's Byrd and Bank Street Ciceros:
Joseph, Bob, and Frank

All night long the capitol glows. The Day-Glo day all night long.
Day-Glo makes the capitol glow makes the capitol glow just like
the globe. To break dawn to break dawn a bridge to cross to break
dawn. All night long all night long the Day-Glo day all night long.
Orange Blaze makes the poster glow makes the poster glow just
like the globe. Between Maryland and Virginia a bridge to cross
between Maryland and Virginia a web of wards. The Day-Glo day
all night long a bridge to cross to break dawn. To break dawn to
break dawn home rule a bridge to cross all night long. Lock this:
the pocket is the sound of the capitol and the sound of the capitol
is a school without walls. A Day-Glo globe all night long. A Day-
Glo poster postering dawn. The light from the posters lasts longer
than the shows. A bridge to cross a percussive map home. A short
conversation between first gear and dawn. A web of wards a severed
map home. Beneath the monuments a baptist chipboard of noise.
Behind the monuments a school without walls. Formerly ten miles
per side formerly ten miles per side. Day-Glo makes the darkness
glow makes the darkness glow just like the globe. A hill and a river
between Maryland and Virginia between Maryland and Virginia a
hill and a river. Song of the District in bits and pieces, a stapled
splatter, proper utensils. Da dee dee dee Da cee cee cee. A short
conversation between hill and bottom. All the ugly people in the
house be quiet. A web of wards a severed map home.

Song of the District in bits and pieces, sirens and synthesizers,
technical difficulties. Da dee dee dee Da cee cee cee. All fat men
free before ten pm. Saturn Yellow makes the poster glow makes
the poster glow just like the globe. Security to the middle of the
pocket between Maryland and Virginia. A y-shaped river, lost in
the city, the staple gun's silver clip of unstitched bridges. Security
to the middle of the pocket between Maryland and Virginia. Work

youngin' work all week and pocket on the weekend. Before a poster disappears it works all week and pockets the weekend. Offset and screened. Twenty-two by thirty-three all week and pocket on the weekend. Before a pocket disappears it works all week and posters the weekend. Offset and screened. Twenty-two by thirty-three all weekend and pocket the weekdays. All night long to poster dawn. Work youngin'. The Day-Glo day stapling home. Splotches of do-it-fluid fluorescence, familiar faces, and lost curfews. The light from the posters lasts longer than the shows. Welcome to Washington, a capitol city, the nation's capitol. To glow national to glow national hot pink and lavender to go national. Day-Glo makes the capitol glow makes the capitol glow just like the globe. The Day-Glo day all night long. All night long all night long. Signal Green makes the Beltway glow makes the Beltway glow just like go-go. The money beltway around Washington won't let glow go won't let go-go glow national. To go national to go national a lightning bolt of trouble to go national. Welcome to Washington, a capitol city, the nation's capitol, already national. All the ugly people in the house (and Senate), please be quiet!

A Psychoalphadiscobetabioaquadoloop

All those
    Liquid love affairs,
Blind swimmers
    Trusting rumps.
We wiggled,
    Imagining water.
Wet, where was
    The One?
Nevermind Atlantis
    And the promise
Of moving pictures,
    A lit candle
In the window
    Of our conscious minds.
Those who danced,
    Pretending to swim
Underwater,
    Did so out
Of pure allegiance.
    Some wore snorkels
Made with
    The waistbands
Of funky underwear,
    Others wet suits
With clothespins
    Clamped to their noses,
Airtight as
    Black Power handshakes.
Rump-by-rump,
    The strings attached
To our thangs were
    Reeled into The Deep

And rhythmic as fins,
　Schools of P signs
Flapped and waved
　Like flags.
One nation
　Under a groove.
No one held their breath
　In the flashlit depth.
No one sank.

Fatal April

Thomas Leon Ellis, Sr. (1945–1991)

The phone rang. It was Doris,
Your sister, calling to say
April had taken you, where,
In your bedroom, when, days ago,
How, murder, no a stroke.

You left a car (but I
Don't drive) and enough cash
In your pockets to buy
A one-way train ticket
From Boston to Washington.

Let's get one thing straight.
I didn't take the money, but
I did take your driver's license
And the Chuck Brown album,
Needle-to-groove,

Round and round,
Where they found you.
Both were metaphors:
The license (I promised, but knew
I'd never get, now I have yours)

And the album because
Of what you may have been
Trying to say about writing,
About home. James keeps
Asking me to visit your grave,

When will I learn to drive
And why I changed my name.
He's your son, stubborn with
An inherited temper. I keep telling him
No, never, there's more than

One way to bury a man.

A Dope Dog Star with Serious Eyes
Versus the Thumpasorus Peoples
(the Thumps Bump)
b/w Brand-New Brand Name

for Dominic Taylor

(The thumps bump
bump the bump bump
bump the thumps bump
bump the bump bump
booty booty)

Side A

In the beginning
There was The One

That didn't wanna
Be called Billy,

So One split
Cause Billy didn't fit
And the void

Bass lit was filled
By a new one—

Bootsy, didn't wanna
Be called William,

So One quit
Cause William tripped
And the void

Bass lit was filled
By another one—

Boogie, didn't wanna
Be called Cordell,

So One broke
Cause Cordell choked
And the void

Bass lit was filled
By the next one—

Skeet, didn't wanna
Be called Rodney,

So One run
Cause Rodney's no fun
And the void

Bass lit was filled
By a sturdy one—

Cherokee, didn't wanna
Be called Jeff,

So One crept
Cause Jeff wasn't def
And the void

Bass lit was filled
By the current one—

Lige, didn't wanna
Be called Curry,

So One listened
Cause Lige sounded different
And the void

Bass lit was filled
By everyone.

Bridge

Blackbyrd's on
    The verge, about
        To lift off,

Fly on. Not since
    The one atop
        The pyramid

Have we witnessed
    An eye in as much
        Heat as Byrd's

—George's fixed
    Third one
        For HBO doesn't

Really count,
    Didn't really bite
        Or bark nights

When Fifi & Pup
Needed roof
Over sucker most.

Bridge

Blackbyrd's gettin'
It on, cloaked in
Scorched skulls,

Fly on. One for
Every beakful
Of bones he's

Unburied and lifted
Back into Space,
Blessed Blackness,

Fly on. Not since
You-Know-Who
Nut his Nubian

And chased us
Up & down alley-
Way have we

Eyewitnessed
So much stray light,
Six black packs,

Bridge

Fly on. A trillion
   Unleashed naps.
      One every starry

Night neck itch
   Told him doo
      Doo your own

Licking rather
   Than sick & set
      And scratch & stare.

B Side

*Papa's got
A brand-new,
Papa's got
A brand-new,
Papa's got
A brand-new,*

Braaaaaaaand—

Maceo, who—
Parker. Any kin
To Charlie,

Who, Parker—
Blow. Any kin
To Ray,

Who Parker—
No. Any kin
To Chan,

Who, Charlie—
Blow. Would you
Buy a shirt

From this man?
No. A b/w television
Or an 8-track tape player

From this man?
Yo. Depends.
What's his name?

Papa's got
A brand-new,
Papa's got
A brand-new,
Papa's got
A brand-new,

Braaaaaaaand—

George, who—
Clinton. Any kin
To Bill,

Who, Clinton—
Blow. Any kin
To Washington,

Who, George—
No. Any kin
To Jefferson,

Who, Clinton—
Blow. Would you
Buy Free Speech

From this man?
No. The right to vote
Or a bucket of wings

From this man?
Yo. Depends. What's
His last name?

*Papa's got
A brand-new,
Papa's got
A brand-new,
Papa's got
A brand-new,*

Braaaaaaaand—

James, who—
Brown. Any kin
To Charlie,

Who, Brown—
Blow. Any kin
To Birmingham,

Who, James—
No. Any kin
To Cleveland,

Who, Brown—
Blow. Would you
Buy a vowel

From this man?
No. A silver spaceship
Parked next to a pyramid

From this man?
Yo. Depends. What's
My man's name again?

*Papa's got
A brand-new,
Papa's got
A brand-new,
Papa's got
A brand-new,*

Braaaaaaaand—

Arsenio, who—
Parker. Any kin
To Pappy,

Who, Parker—
Blow. Any kin
To Pee Wee,

Who, Herman—
No. Any kin
To Ashford,

Who, Simpson—
Blow. Would you
Buy an alibi

From this man?
No. An old jersey
Or the right to remain silent

From this man?
Yo. Depends.
What's his uh?

Papa's got
A brand-new,
Papa's got
A brand-new,
Papa's got
A brand-new,

Brand name.

Tambourine Tommy

More man
Than myth, more myth
Than freak, he would come out
Between bands

In a harness of bells
And high-waters
Held together and up
By a belt of rope.

His skin was thick
As friendship, his spot-lit scalp
Clean as the repaired dome
Of the U.S. Capitol.

Rickety raw
And rickety strong,
He'd run from Barry Farms
To Mount Vernon

With bricks
Borrowed from the wall
Around St. Elizabeths Hospital
In each hand.

There was struggle
In his dance,
Like first-of-the-month
Or Election Day downtown.

His arms tried to
Free Terrance Johnson,
His trickster legs
Rayful Edmond

But such drama
Never made him more
Than spectacle or more
Than beast.

No one thought
Of him as artist,
No one thought
Of him as activist.

His craft, the way
He beat himself
(head, shoulders, knees
and toes), proved he

Was one of us,
A soul searcher
Born and raised
In the District,

Proved he
Could reach in,
Blend, ease before entering,
Proved he

Was our phoenix,
Nobody's Stonestreet,
Part hustler, part athlete,
Tougher than all of Southeast.

SE

Atomic Bride

for Andre Foxxe

A good show
Starts in the
Dressing room

And works its way
To the stage.
Close the door,

Andre's cross-
dressing, what
A drag. All

The world loves
A bride, something
About those gowns.

A good wedding
Starts in the
Department store

And works its way
Into the photo album.
Close the door,

Andre's tying
The knot, what
A drag. Isn't he

Lovely? All
The world loves
A bachelor, some-

thing about glamour
& glitz, white
Shirts, lawsuits.

A good dog
Starts in the yard
And works its way

Into da house.
Close your eyes.
Andre's wide open,

One freak of the week
Per night, what
A drag. Isn't

He lovely? All
The world loves
A nuclear family,

Something about
A suburban home,
Chaos in order.

A good bride starts
In the laboratory
And works his way

To the church.
Close the door,
Andre's thinking

Things over, what
A drag. Isn't
He lovely? All

The world loves
A divorce, something
About broken vows.

A good war starts
In the courtroom
And works its way

To the album cover.
Close the door,
Andre's swearing in,

What a drag.
Isn't he lovely? All
The world loves

A star witness,
Something about
Cross-examination.

A good drug starts
In Washington
And works its way

To the dance floor.
Close the door,
Andre's strung out,

What a drag,
Isn't he lovely? All
The world loves

Rhythm guitar,
Something about
Those warm chords.

A good skeleton
Starts in the closet
And works its way

To the top of the charts.
Start the organ.
Andre's on his way

Down the aisle,
Alone, what an encore. All
The world loves

An explosive ending.
Go ahead, Andre,
Toss the bouquet.

View of the Library of Congress
from Paul Laurence Dunbar High School

for Doris Craig and Michael Olshausen

A white substitute teacher
At an all-Black public high school,
He sought me out saying my poems
Showed promise, range, a gift,
And had I ever heard of T.S. Eliot?
No. Then Robert Hayden perhaps?

Hayden, a former colleague,
Had recently died, and the obituary
He handed me had already begun
Its journey home—from the printed page
Back to tree, gray becoming
Yellow, flower, dirt.

No river, we skipped rocks
On the horizon, above Ground Zero,
From the roof of the Gibson Plaza Apartments.
We'd aim, then shout the names
Of the museums, famous monuments,
And government buildings

Where our grandparents, parents,
Aunts, and uncles worked. Dangerous duds.
The bombs we dropped always fell short,
Missing their mark. No one, not even
Carlton Green who had lived in
As many neighborhoods as me,

Knew in which direction
To launch when I lifted Hayden's
Place of employment—
The Library of Congress—
From the obituary, now folded
In my back pocket, a creased map.

We went home, asked our mothers
But they didn't know. Richard's came
Close: Somewhere near Congress,
On Capitol Hill, take the 30 bus,
Get off before it reaches Anacostia,
Don't cross the bridge into Southeast.

The next day in school
I looked it up—the National Library
Of the United States in Washington, D.C.
Founded in 1800, open to all taxpayers
And citizens. *Snap!* My aunt Doris
Works there, has for years.

Once, on her day off, she
Took me shopping and bought
The dress shoes of my choice.
Loafers. They were dark red,
Almost purple, bruised—the color
of blood before oxygen reaches it.

I was beginning to think
Like a poet, so in my mind
Hayden's dying and my loafers
Were connected, but years apart,
As was Dunbar to other institutions—
Ones I could see, ones I could not.

Practice

for D. W.

A dank, dark basement entered cautiously from the rear.

 The first thing you saw were bass cabinets,

Their enormous backs an unmovable blackness guarding

The door.

 The first thing you heard was feedback and sometimes

Anthony Ross, our manager's kid brother,

Snare- and pedal-less, pretending to kick.

 The floor was worried with slithering cords,

Live wires that lifted and looped like vines of verse.

 The cold brick walls were covered with noise

And, like it or not, several mouth-orange cardboard posters

—those triflin', Day-Glo ones that resemble sores

When the lights are ON, and sores

When they are OFF.

 The air was thick with Chinese takeout, reverb,

The young girls on us, and designer cologne.

 Our roadies recorded and studied us, just in case.

 A microphone slept like an orphan on a dirty pillow

At the bottom of the bass drum's navel-less,

Belly-impersonating, soul-shaped O.

Skin Tight disciplined the congas for not disciplining the bongos

And (sho' you righhht) for not listening:

Bbbridoomp, bbridoomp, bridimp boomp.

Floor tom. Two-faced cymbals. A hint of high-hat.

Sticks.

Our drummer sat facing all of this, caged, while the entire

Frontline (including Karen, our female vocalist) worked out,

Breathing and counting and stepping

Like odd numbers.

Big Earl and Scarecrow stood behind their guitars the same way

The marines at the Tomb of the Unknown Soldier

Stood behind rifles.

The timbales and rototoms, side-by-side, were

Like a finish line of chrome, the bridge (each

And every other groove) a horn's valved prose

Asked for, asked for, asked for.

My Own—Stones

Heads (All Caps), 1989

HEAD UP
HEAD DOWN
HAND UP
HEAD UPSIDE DOWN

HAND UP
HEAD FACING DOWN

HEAD ON TOP
HEAD ON BOTTOM
HEAD TO HEAD

HEAD FACING FRONT
HEAD FACING BACK

STAINED FACE
FACING STAINED
FINGER
STAINED FINGER
FACING STAINED
FACE
STAINED ARMS
BALANCING STAINED
HEADS

WASH FACE
WASH HANDS
WASH HEADS

HEAD FACE UP
HEAD FACE DOWN

FACE WALL
FACE FLOOR

FACE TORTURE
FACE HEAD
ON FINGERS

FACE HEAD
ON HEAD
FACE FINGERS

FACE TONGUE
ON NOSE
FACE DOUBLE SIZE HEADS

FACE SCALP
FACING SCALP

BALANCE HEAD
ON HEAD
BALANCE HEAD
ON HAND

BALANCE TWO HEADS
ON TWO HANDS

NAIL HANDS
HANG HEADS
BREAK ARMS

BALANCE PENCIL
ON PAPER
BUY CATALOG

FACE DEATH
HEAD ON
FACE DOWN

Cowboy Minimalism

for Michelle Weinberg

About twelve
inches or seconds
of pure

pencil is
all any outlaw
needs to draw

both hand
& gun. Most
need less

when the saloon
is cactus
dry

—the whole
town covered-
wagon

dependent. Old
young guns
for hire

dying of
thirst but still
a posse—

& an insider, what
every white
male artist

wants. To be
ridden. To be
horse-like this way,

hung. Why
else go
West—hot on

the pictorial trail
of a woman
never

known for clean
brushes
—when all

of New York
is making
pictures artificial as

REALISM?
Gold Rush. Enough
of false risk

in this age or
any other.
This is

how to draw & how
to show
off. Over-

emphasize gentleness.
Sex exposed. Before
& after

the opening,
Bruce & Susan
take turns in

the saddle,
improvising dripping.
Revolver.

Holster. Revolver.
Barrel &
hole.

Eye shot
point blank with
envy.

Balloon Dog (1993)

for Janeen Moore

Snap. Blow.
Twist. Squeak.
So this is

how—fenced in
by camera
& nightness

—you
got born,
both you

and the cube
coming
into life,

in the white
hands of
some even whiter

-faced clown.
Auguste
aka

dumb-dumb,
the only one capable
of seriously

loving old air & rubber.
Little balloon
dog, totem

-billed one
monitor above
Coffee Spilled,

are you anybody's
best friend?
Your parents

were hands,
cosigners
& you are

you because
your balloon
bones

know you,
ON AIR
& OFF. I paused

when I noticed
your skin had
already

started to
lose shine,
the air inside

your
sausage-linked tubes
escaping

the way poetry escapes
poems that
contain more

ego than
feeling. I feel sorry
for you.

Worse off
than the boy
in the plastic bubble,

you
are bubbles,
all fragmentation

& somebody
else's breath.
Slow Romanticism,

the way love
scenes
hatch.

ASSEMBLAGE
is female. Nothing,
not even

love,
should have to live up to
or as long as

sculpture's attempted
permanence.
Little

balloon dog,
the best your little
balloon heart

can hope for
is silence,
the invisibility

surrounding
the struggle
between

what goes
pop &
art.

T.A.P.O.A.F.O.M.
(The Awesome Power of a Fully Operational Memory)

for Sharan Strange

Alienation

The cassette tape
you sent had a sloppy,
secret second coming on it,
not to mention

the Magic-Markered mugs
of afronauts
with new spaceships
not manufactured

up south
in any of those privately owned,
aspirin-white ghettos
ringworming the ozone.

Thanks! You've been here.
You know what
artist colonization is like:
lunchmeataphobia

and black radioinactive levels
of love amnesia
dense as the cosmos.
A brotherloadless UFO.

Only me and Michael S. Harper.
Barely a sister either,
except Afro-Sappho:
Sapphire.

All of one
day-one month
in the supergroovalistic guerrilla
Nipple Room
and nothing computes.

No wonder they call it Yaddo.
After Faber and Faber
it's the whitest, most minus-da-groove
diaperspace I go:

icka tit,
icka clit,
icka prick,
lickety-split.

Deeper still, I didn't come here to thigh-light
empty memory's bangalang mutiny
to zeep then zapp
glitter's nonlinear reentry.

Anniversary

July 5, 1996. Central Park,
New York City. Both mobs up-in-here,
all of their survivors
and damn-near

half ours: you, me, Vera, Major
and Gelonia as well as
a few extended inkslingers.
I ran into Darius James

(who introduced me
to Pedro Bell) and Tracie Morris,
summer-swimming the crowd.
Pump up and down.

Ah underground angel!
Ah gaps and gadgets!
A limousine arrived from Mars.
Baldass Kabbabie babbled.

Remember? It was November 22, 1986.
I was writing a paper
on Jean Vigo,
and you, Sharan, you were looking

for one of Chris Marker's
films, on video.
Ten years is not a long time
for poetry, but it is for us.

Next we were all living together in Cambridge.
After that, freeing and reading black books.
Then, precious lord, James Baldwin died
and we became a church.

Ah! Those Dark Room Sundays
and their infinite, unrehearsed, double-mouthed
    marches toward the rear.
Some readings you really could hear
a rat piss on cotton

and on off weekends
workshops equally dark and feeling.
Your eloquent *Ash* was promoted there,
    in the funkcronomix,
between memory and experience.

Memory, Walcott says, moves backwards.
If this is true, your memory is a mothership
    minus the disco-sadistic silver
all stars need to shine. Tell the world.
A positive nuisance. Da bomb.

All Their Stanzas Look Alike

All their fences
   All their prisons
All their exercises
   All their agendas
All their stanzas look alike
   All their metaphors
All their bookstores
   All their plantations
All their assassinations
   All their stanzas look alike
All their rejection letters
   All their letters to the editor
All their arts and letters
   All their letters of recommendation
All their stanzas look alike
   All their sexy coverage
All their literary journals
   All their car commercials
All their bribe-spiked blurbs
   All their stanzas look alike
All their favorite writers
   All their writing programs
All their visiting writers
   All their writers-in-residence
All their stanzas look alike
   All their third worlds
All their world series
   All their serial killers
All their killing fields
   All their stanzas look alike
All their state grants
   All their tenure tracks

All their artist colonies
　　All their core faculties
All their stanzas look alike
　　All their Selected Collecteds
All their Oxford Nortons
　　All their Academy Societies
All their Oprah Vendlers
　　All their stanzas look alike
All their haloed holocausts
　　All their coy hetero couplets
All their hollow haloed causes
　　All their tone-deaf tercets
All their stanzas look alike
　　All their tables of contents
All their Poet Laureates
　　All their Ku Klux classics
All their Supreme Court justices
　　Except one, except one
Exceptional one. Exceptional or not,
　　One is not enough.
All their stanzas look alike.
　　Even this, after publication,
Might look alike. Disproves
　　My stereo types.

Groovallegiance

A dream. A democracy. A savage liberty.
And yet another anthem and yet another heaven
and yet another party wants you.
Wants you wants you wants you.
Wants you to funk-a-pen funkapuss.
Wants you to anthologize then re-troop your group.
Wants you to recruit prune juice.
My peeps.
My poetics.
My feet.
All one.
All one.
All one, heel and toe.
My peeps.
My poetics.
My feet.
All one.
All one.
All one, lowly heel and toe.
Br'er feet and br'er beat repeatedly beaten.
Repeatedly beaten repeatedly beaten.
Br'er feet and br'er beat repeatedly beaten.
Repeatedly beaten repeatedly beaten repeatedly beaten.
Br'er feet and br'er beat repeatedly beaten.
Feet feet feet.
Every feet a foot and free, every feet a foot and free,
every feet a foot and free.
A foot and free.
Agony and defeat, a foot and free.
A foot and free.
Every feet a foot and free, every feet a foot and free,
every feet a foot and free.

A foot and free.
Agony and defeat, a foot and free.
Feet feet feet
Reverend feet, a foot and free. Reverend feet,
Repeatedly beaten
Feet feet feet.
A million marchers.
Two parties.
One Washington.
One Washington.
Two parties.
A million marchers.
An afterparty.
An afterparty after marching.
The aftermarch.
An aftermarch-afterparty after marching
all the way to Washington.
Another march another party.
Another aftermarch after another afterparty.
After another afterparty after marching.
After another march afterpartying and after marching
all the way to Washington.
Always Washington always Washington.
Uncle Jam, enjambed
all the way to Washington.
After all that marching after all that partying.
Uncle Jam, enjambed.
Always Washington.
A million marchers.
Two parties.
One Washington.
One Washington.
Two parties.
A million marchers.

Footwork.

If feet work for page shouldn't feet work
for stage, run-on.

Run-on platform.

Run-on floor,
run-on.

If feet work abroad shouldn't feet work
at home, run-on.

Run blood, run-off.

From run flag.

From run bag,
run-on.

Run and tell it.

Run tell tag run tell toe, run tell, tell it.

De-decorate intelligence.

If so also de-decorate form. If so also de-decorate war,
run home.

In every war bloods leave and bloods bleed
and don't come home. What for in every war,
what for, and don't come home.

For war for war for war.

In every war bloods leave and bloods bleed
and don't come home. What for in every war,
what for, and don't come home.

For more for more for more.

That for, in every war.

That for, for every drug.

The war on drugs is a war on bloods,
run tell it.

A line is played. A section plays.

All up, into it, and involved, into it into it
and involved, all up into it and involved.

Footnote.

Take joke.
Take note to toes.
Clip note.
Go home.
Take note to foot.
Race note.
Footnote to feet.
Foot hurt.
Footnote to note.
Cite hurt.
Toe note to foot.
Bottoms up.
Sore foot to church.
Stop running.
If office, if oath.
Broken votes.
A line is played. A section plays.
A protest you press to test repeating itself.
A section plays. A line is played.
A protest you press to test repeating itself.
My peeps.
My poetics.
My feet.
Some ally.
Some enemy.
Mostly tradition.
The jive end.
Br'er rear.
Br'er rear end isms.
Pass out the words.
The kitty is not a toy.
Pass out the words.
The kitty is not a toy.

I owe roots and books to groundwork's underground crosstalk
of African Telephone Churches.
All one all one all one, star-spangled funky.

The Dollar Signs of Autumn

Dip a finger
in a dark viscous substance
and write on the window
of our world. OIL.

Nadine Gordimer

G-R-E-E-D did this.
Greed and Fall, nature's seasonal debris

of brilliant symbolism.
I, too, have prayed for more places to hide

in the shade
between stanzas.

Metaphorically warning students
Workshops are war,
I now wish life would stop imitating life

and that I was talented enough to resist the images
of the S inside the eleven as a hero behind bars.

O but I am not.
The media's cash register of bodies

and the twin terrors at the center of the word dollar
have made me and my craft liar-cowards.

S for September, s for suffering, s for save us.
Damn you, Autumn,
flags are not flowers.

THOMAS SAYERS ELLIS was born and raised in Washington, D.C. He cofounded The Dark Room Collective and received his MFA from Brown University in 1995. His work has appeared widely in magazines and anthologies, and he has received fellowships from the MacDowell Colony, the Fine Arts Work Center, and Yaddo, and a Mrs. Giles Whiting Writers Award. He is the author of *The Good Junk*, which appeared in *Take Three: 1* (Graywolf Press, 1996); a chapbook, *The Genuine Negro Hero* (Kent State University Press, 2001); and a chaplet, *Song On* (WinteRed Press, 2005). *The Maverick Room* was awarded the John C. Zacharis First Book Award. *Skin, Inc.,* his second book, will be published by Graywolf Press in 2010. Currently, Ellis teaches at Sarah Lawrence College and in the Lesley University low-residency MFA program. A photographer and poet, he currently divides his time between Brooklyn, New York, and Washington, D.C.

The Maverick Room has been set in Plantin.
Book design by Wendy Holdman.
Composition by Stanton Publication Services, Inc.
Manufactured by Thomson-Shore on acid-free paper.